STRENGTH FOR LIFE'S BATTLES

Psalms 22: 23-24 (NIV)

You who fear the Lord, praise Him!
All you descendants of Jacob, honor Him!
Revere Him, all you descendants of Israel!

For He has not despised or scorned
the suffering of the afflicted one;
He has not hidden His face from *them*
but has listened to *their* cry for help.

(Author's Emphasis)

STRENGTH

For Life's Battles

MARTINS AKINOLA

COPYRIGHTS

ISBN: 978-0-6481055-4-1

DEDICATION

To every believer going through life's battle.

TABLE OF CONTENTS

PREFACE — vii

ACKNOWLEDGMENTS — viii

INTRODUCTION — 1

ACCIDENTS ARE BETTER PREVENTED — 5

MIND THE APPROACH — 13

THE TRAVAILS OF VICTIMS — 25

LIBERATED BY THE LIGHT — 35

FEELING INADEQUATE — 43

POWERED BY PURPOSE — 53

SEEKING DIVINE HELP — 63

A BRASH DECREE — 73

LOVE FACTOR — 83

DANGER OF RETRIBUTION — 89

THE KING'S STAKE — 95

VALUE OF HUMANS — 101

CONCLUSION — 113

PREFACE

The decision to write this book came naturally and with a lot of excitement. For a season, I studied and preached a series of sermons on a relatively familiar bible passage. Subsequently, I gained a perception of God's viewpoint about human problems and how we can thrive during challenging times.

I have had my share of life's struggles. I have suffered health issues, significant financial losses, loss of loved ones, and had my relationship tested. I thought of sharing with a broader audience the insights gained from the scriptures buttressed with practical experience. And so, I began to write.

This literature demonstrates how challenges are a part of life. It explains how a situation can sometimes worsen when we take the wrong step. The book showcases God's love, the provisions He made for us to recover from adverse experiences, and how we can get hold of the blessings through the Lord Jesus.

As you journey with me through this book, I pray that you gain an assurance that God cares and watches over you. I also pray that you may recover from any previous defeats and gain the courage to do exploits.

ACKNOWLEDGMENTS

Completing this book is indescribably exciting. I attribute the success to God's faithfulness and the support of family and friends.

Praise the Lord for my wife, Anthonia. She encouraged me every step of the way as I put my thoughts into writing. Girl, you are a rare gem.

My sincere gratitude goes to my sons, Christian and Joshua, for their contributions. Indeed, wise children bring joy to their parents.

To my friends, Kenneth Aigbinode and Leanne Curtis, who gladly read the manuscript and provided feedback, I say a big thank you.

INTRODUCTION

The basis for this literature is a short Bible story presented in 1 Kings 3, verses 16 to 28. The account is about Solomon, an ancient king in Israel, and how he vindicated the innocent person when two women brought a complicated case before him. Before going further, I recommend that you read the Bible passage and become acquainted with the narrative, as it teaches a wealth of moral and spiritual lessons.

Regardless of faith, King Solomon is well-known throughout the world. He was the wisest man that ever lived, and he gained his wisdom by requesting it from God.

Solomon took over Israel's rulership from his father (David) and was crowned king at age twenty. Not too long after becoming king, the young ruler offered God a generous burnt offering of a thousand animals. Consequently, in a dream, God asked him to request anything he desired.

Solomon, who presumably understood Israel's significance, made the most of the opportunity offered him. He asked God, not for wealth or other selfish things, but for a discerning heart to govern His people and the ability to distinguish between right and wrong.

The Lord was pleased with Solomon's response, and as a result, He granted him insight in a considerable measure. 1 Kings 4:29 says, "God gave Solomon wisdom and very great insight, and a breadth of understanding as measureless as the sand on the seashore."

Matthew 11:19 says, "…Wisdom is proved right by her deeds." Therefore, we do not recognize a wise person by face value or words, but by action. In other words, we establish someone as prudent when they unravel a puzzle in a manner that shows a sense of sound judgment. Solomon's chance to use this newly bestowed wisdom came when two women in a dispute over a child sought his audience for justice. To the glory of God, he was able to judge the case equitably.

Strictly for this book and to prevent confusion, we will refer to the women in the dispute as Abigail and Dinah.

According to 1 Kings 3:16-28, Abigail and Dinah lived together with no one else sharing their accommodation. It happened that they were both pregnant and delivered their babies three days apart. As Abigail narrated to King Solomon, Dinah accidentally slept over her child and suffocated him. While Abigail was still asleep and under cover of darkness, Dinah swapped her dead child with Abigail's living son.

The reign of King Solomon was from about 970 to 931 BC. Therefore, the dispute between Abigail and her housemate occurred when there was no forensic genotyping, DNA analysis, and fingerprinting. Apart from physical examination, there were no other means to determine who owned the living child. Furthermore, the children involved were very young, making it very difficult to tie them to their rightful mothers.

Seemingly, it was impossible to discern the truth. However, as Solomon cross-examined the women with tact, he figured out that Dinah had lied. So, he returned the living child to Abigail, the rightful mother.

You can imagine the impact of Solomon's judgment on Israel when this incident happened thousands of years ago. The king became renowned among his people and was revered for his wisdom by other nations. The whole nation of Israel was impressed by his verdict and how he arrived at it. The scriptures in 1 Kings 3:28 conclude the narrative by saying, "...They held the king in awe because they saw that he had wisdom from God to administer justice."

As you will learn in the chapters ahead, the story in 1 Kings 3:16-28 might be brief, but it is instructive with contemporary applications. I invite you to relax and enjoy as we illustrate and unpack the lessons.

Chapter 1

ACCIDENTS ARE BETTER PREVENTED

"During the night, this woman's son died because she lay on him." (1 Kings 3:19)

I t is sad to hear about a tragedy where a life is lost. The situation described in the above Bible passage is alarming because the victim was a child. Unfortunately, cases of this kind are a part of life.

Some accidents are preventable when caused by human error, a lack of preventive measures, or a deliberate act of wickedness. There are also times when catastrophic events are inevitable and out of our control, such as natural disasters.

Dinah was unfortunate. Many of us can relate to or imagine her dilemma. She had just survived months of pregnancy and the pains of childbirth. We know that the joy of having a new baby does not negate the physical and emotional changes that come with childbearing. Mothers understand how demanding it is to nurse an infant and how a little sleep can be a luxury during motherhood. Being a single parent whose closest companion was also nursing an infant must have made Dinah's situation particularly dire.

From what we can infer, Dinah did not have a husband. She most likely attended to herself and bore the responsibilities of parenting alone. During her time, there was no form of social security or support from the government for stay-at-home mothers. It must have been challenging for her to take care of herself, provide necessary care for the new-born, and at the same time, meet all their essential needs.

Dinah must have been traumatized after losing her son. She would have been overwhelmed with sorrow, shame, and guilt when she realized the child died because of her mistake. For her dream, pride, and consolation to be irredeemably lost must have been utterly devastating.

Notwithstanding, one could label Dinah as innocently negligent because of the degree of apathy required to sleep over a child until he or she suffocates. We can only imagine the pains the little gem passed through before he finally stopped breathing. If this incident had happened today, Dinah would have been prosecuted and possibly found guilty of negligence or killing the child. Altogether, the child's demise was unfortunate. Preventing it would have been better than managing the aftermath.

The first and most apparent lesson we can gain from Dinah's dilemma is to be conscious of infants' safety and well-being. While many parents can boast of not suffocating their young ones as Dinah did, our careless actions can inflict other forms of damage on the little ones, some of which can leave them virtually lifeless.

People with significant emotional baggage caused by a lack of parental care have become the norm in our societies. Many people dress, act, and speak as if they are doing well. Often, we find them broken inside when we pry.

Parents and guardians influence their children and wards more than they often assumed. Adults are the single most significant examples for their offspring. When we expose the vulnerable generation to dangerous vices and immoral practices, we are harming them, and they stand the risk of having a shortchanged future.

Children who survive abuse and neglect are often scarred, sometimes for life. On the other hand, those who enjoyed good parenting generally have a better chance to excel in life. They are more likely to have sound mental health, a cheerful disposition, and fewer behavioral problems.

For the people of faith, parenting is not all about physical support. The scriptures challenge us to facilitate our offspring's relationship with the Lord. We may take consolation that children can grow to discover God independently, but a good foundation laid by parents or guardians can be helpful. When we commit to walking with God, the children are likely to follow suit. Otherwise, we stand the risk of suffocating our children spiritually, putting them at the risk of neglecting God or denying His existence. The biblical instruction in Proverbs 22:6 is to "start children off on the way they should go, and even when they are old, they will not turn from it."

As responsible parents and guardians, let us strive to make decisions in our children's best interests. Let us be intentional in the drive to be role models. What our children learn before they reach the age of rebellion would support them through the trying period.

Mark 8:36-37 says, "What good is it for someone to gain the whole world, yet forfeit their soul? Or what can anyone give in exchange for their soul?" Jesus emphasized in this Bible passage why we should take seriously our spirituality and that of our kids. In my opinion, reverence for God is the most significant legacy any parent can leave for their children.

Moreover, children are not the only blessing from God. The charge to safeguard our gifts concerns us all, irrespective of age or social status. The most fundamental of our benefits, our life, and the body that houses it is a unique gift. As an expression of gratitude to God, let us abstain from habits that are detrimental to our well-being lest we sleep over the precious gift and destroy it.

The people around us, those we come across in our day to day lives, are priceless. I urge you not to isolate yourself mentally or socially, forfeiting the benefits of having relationships. A good relationship is an invaluable treasure from God. Those who have friends or family members should cherish them. If you have companions who share in your joy or wipe your tears, please appreciate them.

Letting people who care for us know how much we appreciate them fosters relationships and is profitable to the community. Just imagine how pleased you were the last time someone showed you an act of gratitude. You probably felt appreciated, thought your effort worthwhile, and looked forward to helping again.

We can quickly get caught up in the hustle-and-bustle of life such that we neglect the gifts God provided through our loved ones. I tend to take life too seriously and overwork myself. On the opposite end of the spectrum is my wife, who is more disciplined with work and creates time for fun. Ironically, my initial interpretation of her personality was someone who wasted precious time. Meanwhile, she believed my lifestyle was not sustainable. The clash in mentality generated a lot of friction at the early stage of our marriage, and it took us a while to accept that God designed us to complement each other.

After a series of sharp disagreements, God opened our eyes to the truth about our differences. My wife had a particular dream which challenged us. We interpreted the vision as God telling us to accommodate each other and take advantage of the differences instead of hindering ourselves and jeopardizing our future. The insight from the dream changed our perceptions about relationships.

Subsequently, we became more open and trusting, which developed to accepting our shortcomings and validating each other more. It became apparent that, like Dinah, we were choking the life out of our blessings before God intervened. Still, being human, we continue to have moments when we disagree, but our adjustment mechanism assures harmony.

Our talents, expertise, and the opportunities associated with them are precious blessings that need safeguarding. There is a danger when we invest time and resources to learn a trade or a skill but settle for a job with minimal challenges. This attitude causes mediocrity and defeats the purpose for which we learned the skills.

We should never stop learning lest we stop growing and become redundant in our professions. The world is continually evolving, with new technologies replacing the old. Those who would thrive and be relevant in the job market must adopt a lifelong learning disposition.

Dear friend, we do not merit the blessings God bestowed on us but obtain them by grace. While we are undeserving, He blesses us with invaluable benefits. Let us be accountable and safeguard these gifts jealously. Nurturing and preserving our blessings are usually worthwhile, especially compared to the devastation of losing them. The old saying, 'Prevention is better than cure,' is always a piece of sound advice. I urge you to activate and catalyze your natural and spiritual abilities. Treasure and nurse them to maturity.

My sincere condolences go out to those who can relate to Dinah, especially people who have accidentally lost a precious gift. From personal experience, the pain can be unbearable and considerably worse when the loss is due to our negligence. Nonetheless, I encourage not to lose hope but ask God to restore the lost fortunes and comfort us in the way He knows best.

As we would learn in the chapters ahead, God's love for us is deep and tender. He understands we are human and prone to mistakes. He does not despise or scorn the suffering of the afflicted one. Instead, He hastens to rescue the broken-hearted who seeks Him for help.

1. We are encouraged to safeguard the blessings God freely lavished on us. What are the natural and spiritual gifts of yours that are worth protecting?

2. What is the significance of a healthy lifestyle, and how can we maintain it?

3. How does our walk with God impact the people around us?

4. Our talents, expertise, and the opportunities associated with them are gifts from God. What practical steps are you taking to protect yours?

5. The people in our community are an invaluable treasure from God. Give examples of how we can make the most of the privilege.

BIBLE READINGS

Proverbs 12:11

Mark 8:36-37

Ephesians 5:15-17

SEEK | **FIND** | **GROW IN GRACE**

Chapter 2

MIND THE APPROACH

"So she got up in the middle of the night and took my son from my side while I your servant was asleep. She put him by her breast and put her dead son by my breast." (1 king 3:20)

In the above Bible passage, Abigail narrated how, while she was asleep, Dinah used the cover of darkness to swap her dead child with Abigail's living son.

After attempting to exploit sleeping Abigail, it would be understandable if anyone regarded Dinah as remorseless, wicked, and morally deficient. After all, she displayed no sense of responsibility or consideration for herself or her roommate. She became so desperate to relieve herself of the self-inflicted misery that she victimized her vulnerable neighbor.

Rationalizing the irrational

There are indications that Dinah's actions after discovering her son's death were deliberate. It takes conscious effort to conceptualize, plan, and execute the scheme she unleashed on her neighbor. Regardless, examining the story from her position reveals a desperate bereaved mother, someone whose emotions spiraled into a state of despair after losing a precious gift instead of a heartless swindler.

The concept of losing a loved one alone is heartbreaking, not to mention when this happens suddenly. The pain caused can then become unbearable and extremely traumatic. Unfortunately, some people find consolation in blaming others for their situation. In Dinah's case, the accident was sudden, she suffered an irreversible loss, and she was solely and personally responsible for the incident. These factors must have caused a radical shift in her reasoning, ultimately resulting in the decision to exploit Abigail's vulnerability.

Given the situation she found herself in, is it justifiable to blame Dinah? Can we condemn her when we all have panicked and taken steps that we ordinarily would not have considered? Or, was her dishonesty justified because she was traumatized?

The essence of this chapter is neither to condemn nor to exonerate Dinah. Instead, we want to examine factors contributing to her behavior and understand how we naturally respond when confronted with a similar dilemma. Furthermore, we will analyze what she could have done differently and explore a more prudent and conscientious approach to such situations.

Fear, panic, and anxiety are inherent in human beings. They are a natural part of our survival instinct. We are bound to experience a measure of these feelings at any given moment in our lives. It is possible to become uncontrollably fearful and anxious when we make serious mistakes. These feelings can disrupt our decision-making processes. They can set in motion spontaneous and unwarranted reactions that we may find incomprehensible and embarrassing when we review our actions.

The inability to see another workable solution contributed to Dinah's insensitive choice after discovering she had accidentally killed her child. Consequently, she succumbed to instinct rather than good judgment and yielded to fear rather than faith.

When unable to find a practical solution to challenges, we can become agitated, calculating, and desperate. Conversely, we feel a sense of relief when we discern the way forward. It is not necessarily the level of difficulty confronting us momentarily that makes us apprehensive but how to overcome the immediate challenge.

Proverbs 13:12 says, "Hope deferred makes the heart sick…" People who give up hope may struggle to hang on to life. Unless there is an intervention, they can degenerate into wreaking havoc on their own lives or endanger others.

We are better armed to survive

Based on the evidence from the Bible passage, Dinah's options were limited and called for a strong moral fiber. The incident which led to her son's demise happened at night. There was no emergency communication means like the phones and internet services we so heavily rely on today during her time. Besides the rich people who rode on horses, camels, donkeys, or carts mounted on these animals, most people in that era trekked, which constrained mobility.

It must have been a considerable task for Dinah to contact anyone living longer than a few yards when the emergency occurred. Those from whom she could have sought support were fewer still, in a group consisting of her roommate, neighbors, and perhaps, relatives. Unfortunately, none of these people were obliged to provide her assistance with a dead child.

The world we live in is much more advanced in technology than in Dinah's time. We have alternative means to seek help, be it during the day or night, and across geographical boundaries. We can access the Internet and get the world's attention if the situation demands it.

Today, someone can send an SOS from a remote location and move the world to plan a rescue if the cause is justifiable. Many communities now have people trained and responsible for providing aid to those in desperate need, including victims of self-inflicted negligence like Dinah.

The potential to pull through hard times has drastically increased over time. Notwithstanding, individuals who devise contingency plans before disaster strikes always have a better chance of survival. At the very least, it is advisable to be acquainted with contact information to humanitarian and emergency services in our community. They can be lifesavers when disaster strikes.

Most victims of accidents rarely envision a threat until tragedy strikes. Knowing the steps to take and the people to contact in an emergency will prevent us from acting under stress and buttress our hope. When we plan, we can approach critical matters with adequate information and make decisions based on a strong foundation and sound judgment.

A taste of the unexpected

To remain hopeful in a problematic situation requires trusting something or someone reliable and predictable. Over the years, I have continued to find solace in God whenever I am in distress. In August 2017, I got a phone call from my son's school. It was one of those calls every parent dreads. My son was involved in an accident and needed emergency treatment.

The fact that the staff who contacted me was calm while delivering the message did not help. I knew such people trained professionally to communicate bad news. For that reason, my knowledge was counterproductive, and it only increased my worries. I was overwhelmed with the concern that my son's condition could be more severe than the staff sounded. Fear and anxiety got hold of me as I thought of the accident's possible implications.

We were living approximately five kilometers away from my son's school. Nevertheless, the journey seemed like an eternity despite the light traffic along the way. I would have put myself together better if my wife (who has a medical background) had accompanied me. Unfortunately, she had worked overnight and returned that morning and was asleep when the call came.

I was still on the way to my son's school when God gave me a weapon against my fears - His word and the testimony of His faithfulness. The verse of the scriptures that came to mind was Psalms 112:7. The Bible says in that verse, "They will have no fear of bad news; their hearts are steadfast, trusting in the Lord." From this scripture, I learned that while sad news may abound, I need to be steadfast in trusting God.

It was not the first time my son would sustain an injury that required an immediate surgical operation. It was sad that we had to go through the awful experience all over. However, the testimony of God's faithfulness in the previous instance gave me the much-needed strength and courage to trust Him on this second occasion.

I said to myself, "He knows about this situation; He delivered me in the past. He will do it again." In all sincerity, though I trusted God in my heart, my body was weak due to the shock. I was physically shaking until I got to my son's school.

Seeing my son conscious a moment later gave me a powerful sense of relief. As the paramedics briefed me about the cause and the preliminary assessments of the wounds, I continued to trust God for a total recovery. Knowing that we had competent surgeons in the city who could perform the required surgical operation calmed my nerves further.

Moreover, my son was about to start a tortuous recovery journey, which would impact the boy and us as his parents. The pains from the injuries, the trauma of surgical operation, and the hospital bed restriction were just a few of the immediate challenges. Besides, our daily routine would have to change to accommodate our new reality.

For my son, the inability to use his body was disheartening. He had no choice but to depend on others.

Caregivers at the hospital, friends, and family members became indispensable. Due to his condition, he reluctantly relaxed his privacy. The psychological impact of doing so was significant. Being a sportsman who adores playing basketball meant he missed an invaluable source of motivation. He was partially immobilized and confined to the bed for a season. Unfortunately, this implies he stopped going to school and could not connect with his friends.

The activities he could partake in were limited, which made him sad and subsequently depressed. Computer games and other indoor activities that ordinarily cheer him up became exhausting. We noticed changes in his attitude as he developed a pessimistic view of himself and frequently recalled the similar accident he had twelve months earlier.

The distress from the above event would have been worse without God's reassurance and supports from family and friends. Fear and anxiety could have made me drive to the school in an unsafe manner. Without courage from God and the testimony of His goodness, perhaps I would have been less courteous with the medical staff I met at the scene. But with God's help, we were able to support my son when he needed us most.

A few words of caution

When Dinah chose to cover up her wrong and victimize her neighbor, she began an uphill battle. One can only imagine the shame after King Solomon exposed her lies.

She had the opportunity to amend her ways when Abigail confronted her but refused until she became a criminal before the law.

From the moment Dinah chose to exploit Abigail, she ceased to be a victim and became a culprit. The step led to more regret and further isolation. Those who ordinarily would have empathized with her as a grieving mother then had reasons to question her integrity. By resorting to deceit, she forfeited the compassion she would have received if she had been truthful.

When faced with critical setbacks, the initial choices matter more than the afterthoughts. It is normal to be jittery and perhaps unable to think straight when we feel insecure. Notwithstanding, our inability to see a way out of a problem does not mean there is no way. It only highlights our limitations.

Besides, when we continue too long in the wrong direction, it becomes harder to change course. When we adopt a wrong path, we stand the risk of drifting away from God's plan and walking into the enemy's trap. Taking the wrong approach in a bad situation can only make matters worse.

The enemy seeks to take advantage of us when we are most vulnerable. He likes to magnify problems out of proportion to weaken our defenses and make us concede defeat. We must be vigilant. Satan will tempt us with ridiculous options as 'shortcuts.' While his suggestions may appear to be advantageous, his intentions are usually cruel as he is incapable of doing good. The Bible in John

10:10 confirms his mission, which is to steal, kill, and destroy.

Every believer is entitled to hope in God during dire situations. We can trust Him with confidence because He created the earth and is in full control of it. The tomorrow that suddenly seems vague to us is vivid in His eyes. Our God lives outside of time and knows the end from the beginning. He is willing to act on our behalf and change things to favor us.

Someone may ask, "What could Dinah hope for in God after her son had died?" After losing a child in the year 2000, my wife and I went through the darkest cloud of sadness we have ever experienced. To hold a lifeless child in our hands is not something any parent can forget easily. There was the feeling of "What could we have done differently? What signal did we miss from the Lord and failed to respond to promptly; what message did we neglect?"

Initially, we hoped for the child to come back to life, which did not materialize. With encouragement from friends and loved ones, we resolved to look up to God, the Giver of the child, for comfort. After a period of grief, He graciously blessed us with another child.

Dear friend, sad and unfortunate incidents are real, and they are a part of life in our fallen world. Through my distress, I learned how God's thoughts could be different from ours. His ways are far beyond anything we can visualize. Therefore, I urge those going through challenging situations to embrace a godly approach. We can believe in the miraculous and providence even when all the odds are against us. With God on our side, we will pull through tempest ordeals.

1. Share experience and afterthought of an occasion when you took steps you ordinarily would not have considered.

2. We risk making a poor judgment when we are instinctual, yet the disposition can motivate a prompt response to threats. Discuss the pros and cons of being instinctual.

3. Share an experience when you over-prepared or underprepared for an emergency.

4. How conversant are you with the emergency services in your community and their contacts?

5. How do we ensure fear, panic, and anxiety do not have the best of us or complicate a bad situation?

BIBLE READINGS

2 Timothy 1:7

Proverbs 3:5-6

Proverbs 14:12

Proverbs 19:2

SEEK   FIND   GROW IN GRACE

Chapter 3

THE TRAVAILS OF VICTIMS

"So she got up in the middle of the night and took my son from my side while I your servant was asleep. She put him by her breast and put her dead son by my breast." (1 Kings 3:20)

Abigail was a victim of Dinah's mistake. If not for Dinah, Abigail would not have suffered the initial trauma of grieving, the hassles of petitioning King Solomon for justice, and the embarrassment of discussing her private matters in public.

Dinah was about to cost Abigail her son, her joy, and her pride before King Solomon intervened. If Abigail had failed in her appeal, the public would never know the truth, and they could blame her for a crime she did not commit. She was fortunate the king judged rightly, as she risked losing her self-worth and retaining a sense of failure as a parent.

Like Abigail, many innocent people go through hardships and difficulties because of the actions of others. Victims of abuse, violence, and neglect are regular people who were on course to realizing their dreams until someone else destroyed them.

A victim's struggle can be physical, emotional, psychological, or practical. Tragedies can leave scars and injuries that make people partially or entirely disabled. It forces victims to rely on other people to do tasks they were once able to do without assistance. To be pitied and looked down on as someone who needs charity can erode our self-confidence. Moreover, the concept of becoming a burden to loved ones and the public can further agitate fragile emotional and mental states.

Many are the afflictions of victims. Those who go through scary incidents can suffer from the typical symptoms of post-traumatic stress disorder, including nightmares, flashbacks, agitation, anxiety, depression, and an inability to confront specific situations. Besides, we all can become fearful when we foresee a bleak future. So, tragedies can trigger uncertainties and drive victims to the extremes, resenting themselves, the people who caused them harm, those who ought to have prevented the incident, or even humanity as a whole.

Road to recovery

Surviving in the psychological landscape of a victim can be a daunting task. Success is dependent on the severity of the case, an individual's will-power, and available resources. Factors like nationality and where the incident occurred may also become significant. For example, it is easier to survive as a victim in developed countries than in nations with weak human rights, inadequate medical facilities, or a lack of a suitable support system. The road to recovery is never easy, even when the resources are readily available.

In Abigail's case, taking legal action was appropriate. The incident occurred within Solomon's jurisdiction, her issue was genuine and salvageable, and she had free access to a king who could administer justice. Whenever the situation demands it, let us take legal actions against people who harm us. Claiming compensations may not mend a broken heart or make up for losses, but it will help hold offenders accountable for their negligence.

Abigail might not have been aware of the impact of her story on the public. Her choices contributed to the credit King Solomon received for the judgment. She was selfless in her willingness to let the surviving child live. I hope she recognized afterward that her courage to pursue justice motivated many in Israel and glorified God. Moreover, her approach and tenacity have continued to be a moral influence on generations after her.

I encourage victims to narrate their encounters to the right audience. Creating public awareness can facilitate recovery and give victims a sense of relevance. It can prevent the innocent from experiencing similar fates and break down stigmas. Many breakthroughs in fighting sexual abuse, domestic violence, and human trafficking started with someone daring to speak up and present the issue before the appropriate authorities.

Another reason to share our story is to attract help. When the atmosphere is right, let us share our stories with a positive attitude and good intentions. It can draw attention and motivate the public to support our rehabilitation efforts. Our help comes from the Lord. Notwithstanding, He may choose to touch the hearts of fellow humans for our good.

My story

In 2012, I struggled to have a positive attitude after falling victim to poor judgment at the workplace. After taking over the management of a project, I noticed we did not budget for a crucial piece of data needed for its successful execution. The ramification was that the project would cost significantly more than previously presented to the company's management.

Everyone appreciated that the finding would save the company from a poor investment decision. On the other hand, my manager and colleagues - the people responsible for oversight - were worried about their careers. There and then, I found myself in the center of a controversy.

The above incident continued for months, and suddenly I was perceived to be a black sheep that many colleagues tried to avoid. I found myself responding to this frustrating experience with anger. At one point, I nearly snapped while in a meeting with my manager and his boss. I was disappointed in their insincerity and how they played workplace politics despite knowing the truth. I felt exploited as they asked me questions to which they ought to provide answers for the company.

Sadly, the bureaucracy went on for months. In the end, I was penalized and nearly lost my job because I could not persuade the Director to approve the additional funding needed to acquire the omitted data. I was overwhelmed but recovered reasonably well from the above incident, perhaps due to the lessons learned from a previous one.

A year earlier, I got entangled in a separate work-related saga. It was a typical example of being in the wrong place at the wrong time. I could not blame anyone for it, but it cost me self-confidence, and I subsequently went into a state of depression.

I have always loved my job and enjoyed dressing corporately. On this occasion, it was as if the whole world was against me. I could not care less and only wore clothes to suit my state of despair. My frustration did not stop at the office. It extended home and became apparent in how I interacted at the church. I grew susceptible and easily agitated because I could not get over my stress.

I continued struggling until I discovered that my wife had developed a health issue but would not discuss it. She was worried that my condition might deteriorate if she involved me in her situation. Then, I knew I had to change my attitude as I risked losing everything I ever valued, especially my family.

Subsequently, my wife and I took the first significant step by having a heart-to-heart talk. We recognized that the issues at work had impacted us more than we thought. We identified the potential long-term effect on our relationships, our loved ones, especially our children. After examining all possibilities, we acknowledged the privilege of having a stable job but concluded that we were ready to sacrifice it, if necessary, to save our family.

Comfort through relationships

I did not take legal action against my employer in the encounters narrated above. I thought it would be inappropriate and somewhat of an overkill for the circumstances. Being a devoted family man with a wife and two adorable children provided me some comfort as I roamed the dark and lonely road.

Besides, I found solace in sharing my story with my friends and associates, especially those who shared my values. The testimonies and words of encouragement from survivors of similar situations were priceless. It acted as a form of therapy, boosting my confidence, and stirred me up to hope for a future. Without my family and dependable friends, I would have struggled longer than I did. The aftermath of the incidents would also have been far worse.

A good relationship is a treasure that believers should never lack. The people with intimate relationships have a better chance of surviving as victims than those who isolate themselves. To conncct with the people around us, starting with our immediate family, is beneficial. They are usually the ones who are obliged to come to our aid and show genuine empathy when we are in distress.

Dear friend, I encourage you to build up your relationships and continue to make new ones. The more people in your network of friends, the lighter the burden of tough times will be for everyone. No one is waiting for us to run into trouble so that they might help. Those who support us have their days planned out but reprioritize to accommodate us out of love. If we have only a few individuals within reach, the demand to assist may overwhelm them.

We may suffer unnecessarily after falling victim because of a lack of helping hands. Those who live in privacy and isolation may struggle when disaster strikes. God never designed man to be alone or to be lonely. Ecclesiastes 4:12 says that a three-strand cord is not quickly broken in. We are always safer when we band together like a solid fence. Perhaps, if Abigail and Dinah had been within a supportive family structure, the incident and fallouts would have been mitigated.

The grace to trust is fading away in our society. Mutual and harmonious relationships where people genuinely relate and care for each other is declining, even in the Church. Whereas individualism, the drive for independence and self-reliance, is gaining ground and setting a precedent for a generation rooted in isolationism. In this respect, we should not allow information and communication technologies, as valuable as they are today, to replace authentic and caring companionships.

I urge you to connect with people beyond social media and church events. Let us build trust and invest in relationships. There is no relationship when there is no trust. But when we believe in people, we earn their confidence and, subsequently, their commitment. Those who go through trials alone are vulnerable to evil thoughts, emotional breakdowns, and impulses. They are at risk of falling prey to the Enemy.

All in all, tragedies may leave a bleak outlook in their wake. There is a tendency to take a passive or despairing view of life while tough times persist. When we have the choice, let us embrace hope and choose to rebuild rather than self-pity. Victim mentality is more comfortable to adopt than to reject. We must avoid becoming trapped in mindsets that are a threshold for damaging consequences.

1. Give examples of the typical difficulties that victims face?

2. Why should victims share their stories and create public awareness?

3. What are the typical signs of victim-mentality, consequences of the disposition, and how can we avoid getting trapped in it?

4. Given biblical injunctions, under what circumstances can we take legal action against a victimizer?

5. How easy do you get along with people around you? Who are you likely to contact during an emergency? Why do you choose them?

BIBLE READINGS

Matthew
5:25

Psalms
10:14
9:9-10

Proverbs
29:7

ICorinthians
6:5-6

SEEK | **FIND** | **GROW IN GRACE**

Chapter 4

LIBERATED BY THE LIGHT

"The next morning, I got up to nurse my son—and he was dead! But when I looked at him closely in the morning light, I saw that it was not the son I had borne." (1 Kings 3:21)

he previous chapter examined how Dinah swapped her dead child with Abigail's living one. As we learn from the above Bible passage, when Abigail woke up the next morning and looked closely, she recognized that the child lying dead by her breast was not the one she bore.

Abigail must have panicked, becoming grieved, ashamed, and guilt-stricken over her negligence before discovering the truth. The mourning would have continued until she realized the dead child was not hers, and his death could not have been her fault.

Abigail eventually recovered from her ordeal, but the story would have been different but for the light that exposed her desperate housemate's deceit. Dinah had capitalized on darkness to perpetuate her bad intentions, but the morning light gave her up and allowed Abigail to re-examine her situation.

In the brightness of the morning, Abigail gained insight into knowledge Dinah obscured under darkness. The fresh insight aroused Abigail's confidence and made her believe something positive could still happen. She then had reasons to contend with the adversary instead of wallowing in misery.

If Abigail had examined the dead child in the dark, she would not have noticed the difference. Without the light, she would have concurred to the lies of the wicked one. Abigail would not have visualized or explored the chance to recover from her oppressor save for the divinely timed, morning-induced illumination. Concisely, the light motivated Abigail's first glimpse of hope to recover from Dinah's attack.

Before the morning light assisted Abigail, we observed a demonstration of the limitations in human knowledge, wisdom, and emotions. Our natural senses are bound to fall short under certain circumstances. Therefore, we need divine assistance if we must discern situations correctly and explore all the possibilities.

God can relate to the feelings of victims. He knows how information that offers hope can be a lifeline to someone saddled with discouragement. In His kindness, He created the morning light and made it shine at the appointed time to liberate Abigail, an unfortunate woman.

The Bible says, "God's word is a lamp for our feet and a light on our path" (Psalms 119:105). In God's word, we have an illumination superior to the morning light that liberated Abigail. While Abigail waited until sunrise before unearthing the deceiver's trick, times and seasons do not restrict God's word. It is always near us, day and night. It is reliable today, tomorrow, and forever.

God is wiser than humans, and His word is unwavering. "For the word of God is alive and active. Sharper than any double-edged sword, it penetrates even to dividing soul and spirit, joints, and marrow; it judges the heart's thoughts and attitudes. Nothing in all of creation is hidden from God's sight. Everything is uncovered and laid bare before the eyes of him to whom we must give account" Hebrews 4:12-13.

From personal experience, every victim desires to know what caused them misfortune and what their future holds. The time of crisis is not a time for speculation. Victims want answers to the deep questions in their hearts. If there is any promise of hope, victims want it reliable and sustainable. They want to capitalize on the opportunity to regain their lives and do it quickly before the chance escapes them.

At this point, God's word, His counsel, and verdict become indispensable because He is the supreme authority over every matter. God is the only one who knows what tomorrow holds and has answers to the questions in the hearts of all humans. His guidance is dependable and superior to any other source.

We have witnessed many charming and inspiring helpers, but none guarantees or backs up their word like our God. He follows through His promises and fulfills them at the appointed times when we meet our part of the bargain. As Luke 1:37 puts it, "For no word from God will ever fail." What an inspiration, comfort, and assurance from God's word!

Abigail's success explains why we liken knowledge to power, wealth, and treasure. When we are well informed, we have the basis to act confidently and promptly. The deeper the understanding of God's counsel, the better equipped we are to taking the right steps and solving problems.

Abigail's disposition after knowing the truth shows how God's word can sway a victim's morale. It changes the countenance from fear to faith and despair to hope. Can you imagine Abigail's fate without the enlightenment gained through the light? It is a destiny loaded with hopelessness, undue pain, regrets, self-pity, shame, confusion, and perhaps death.

No one meaningfully engages in a mission with an end they cannot see. Conversely, we gain boldness to chase dreams when we foresee possibilities. The more God's word is in us, the more illuminated our heart is, the more enlightened we will be about His promises, and the more we can petition Him with confidence.

I once witnessed a six-year-old asking her mother for bread. The mother sarcastically answered, "There is no more, you have finished the bread." The little girl responded as she walked towards the fridge, saying, "Mom, you mean you do not want to see the bread in the refrigerator?" "Come, I will show you."

The kid in that story was as funny as she was intelligent. She challenged my faith as her actions demonstrated how knowledge empowers our minds to ask bravely and with expectations in prayers. The little girl would not back off because she was sure there was bread in the fridge. She respected her mother's position, but the awareness of the truth compelled her to insist on her demand. You can guess what happened in the end. The mother laughed, gave her the bread, and everyone present recognized she earned the reward. Moreover, the mother was proud to have such a clever daughter.

Usually, we do not ask in prayers more than what we know God can provide. Those familiar with the boundless treasures in His storeroom will find grace to wait on Him. They will remain steadfast in their quest for blessings and until He turns their situation around for good.

I encourage you to regularly read the scriptures and find out what God has to say concerning you. He may also reveal His counsel through divine revelations such as dreams, visions, or a word of prophecy. If God chooses any means other than the scriptures, my advice is to test the instruction and ensure it aligns with the scriptures.

Moreover, Abigail explained to King Solomon how she looked at the dead child "closely" in the morning light. Her tenacity is not unusual for a mother who lost her son and desperately needs consolation. Anything less than a purposeful assessment of the child she found by her breast would not have yielded the revelation she got.

To assess our situation in the light of God's word requires time and dedication. James 1:25 says, "But whoever looks *intently* into the perfect law that gives freedom and continues in it-not forgetting what they have heard, but doing it—they will be blessed in what they do" (author's emphasis). We need to be intentional about knowing what God says, especially when something significant to us is at risk.

We know Dinah did not hand over the living child despite Abigail's firm conviction. It is fair to say the morning light did not give Abigail a breakthrough outrightly, but it inspired her to fight until she secured her much-needed deliverance. God's word will reveal His intentions and provide us with direction. We must act on the leading for our breakthrough to materialize.

Do you have a vision, dream, or a word of prophecy that promised hope? Does a revelation from the scriptures inspire you? Be careful to search out and discover the meaning, the direction it offers, and follow-through. Typically, God's word provides us reasons to be thankful, something to pray about, a sin to confess, an attitude to stop or develop, or a promise to claim.

1. How did daylight inspire Abigail to recover from Dinah's deceit?

2. Through what means can we know God's mind concerning us?

3. Share an experience when you sought and discovered God's will concerning a matter.

4. How do we ensure a word of prophecy, dream, or a piece of advice from a friend aligns with the scriptures before taking it as God's word?

5. Share an experience when God's word inspired hope in you to pursue a dream.

BIBLE READINGS

Psalms 119:105,162

Luke 1:37

1 John 1:7

Matthew 6:22-23

SEEK **FIND** **GROW IN GRACE**

Chapter 5

FEELING INADEQUATE

Now two prostitutes came to the king and stood before him.
(1 Kings 3:16)

Anyone who can relate to Abigail's struggle would applaud her bravery in pursuing an audience with King Solomon. It takes courage to chase a goal when we lack the qualifications or practical knowledge to succeed.

This chapter examines the inner struggles Abigail overcame before seeking Solomon's intervention. We will compare her experience to what we are likely to encounter when facing a similar situation in the present day.

As much as the royal standard was concerned, Abigail was in no state to stand before Solomon. She was a single mother and a commoner and would not be familiar with royal protocols. In Abigail's time, women went into prostitution because they lacked relatives who could support them. Women of her standing were borderline illegal and often subject to abuse. In society's eyes, Abigail's life had less meaning than the average person. She would have worried about how the audience would perceive her during the hearing.

For Abigail to be a prostitute meant she would not have had a good education and most likely lacked the competence to articulate her case or defend herself. Unlike today where the government provides lawyers to those who cannot afford a private attorney, Abigail would have worried about being in Solomon's court with no one to protect her interests or give moral support.

Before approaching the king, Abigail would have had to handle the most crippling obstacle of all, her guilt. As a mother, the fact that she slumbered so deeply and did not notice when Dinah swapped the children would have weighed heavily on her conscience. Nobody takes delight in discussing private and unpleasant matters about themselves in public. The idea of Abigail telling the most embarrassing story of her life in the open would not have helped her mood.

Furthermore, since the court system's inauguration, the justice system has functioned with the basis of proof, whereby a defender and the accuser are required to provide evidence to support their plea. In Abigail's situation, there was no third-party witness of the event, and she had no convincing proof that the living child was hers. Other than her words, which Dinah had refuted, Abigail had no evidence to support the claim that the baby was hers.

Abigail's situation seemed doomed, and her opponent's stance would not have encouraged her either. Dinah had an overwhelming amount of time to firm up her position. While Abigail was asleep, she planned and executed her scheme. She denied the accusation at home and remained unfazed as she continued to defend her standpoint before King Solomon.

Abigail's fear would have produced a scenario where the case went against her. The possibility of losing the child to the opponent is heartbreaking, but the consequences could be lethal if she were found guilty. As with most monarchs, the king's ruling was final, and with no higher authority to hear an appeal. All in all, when Abigail decided to face Solomon's courtroom, she would have been a broken woman whose life relied solely on the king's intuition and sense of justice.

Centuries have passed since Abigail fought to retain her child, but the struggles we face while chasing our dreams or claiming our possessions are just as daunting. Like Abigail, we may feel unworthy, unprepared, unqualified, guilty, inferior, and weary of the enemy. These factors can threaten our confidence and make recovery tasks overwhelming. Abigail gained back what was rightfully hers despite the presumably slim chance of success. For her to succeed proves we can thrive regardless of our insufficiency.

The previous events in Abigail's lives would have influenced her misgivings about approaching King Solomon. Victims are prone to developing a cynical mindset and may find it challenging to fit into a liberal society or lifestyle. We are a product of our experiences. As a result, whatever we pass through in life determines how we think inwardly and the personality that we manifest outwardly.

As a child, I lived in rural communities until I gained admission to the university. The limited exposure made me suffer social anxiety and insecurity when I relocated to the city for tertiary education. Without any form of discrimination against me, I felt like the entire world was staring at me with pity. It was as if my imperfections were written on a plaque and hung on my neck. The pessimistic viewpoint impacted my conduct, and I soon developed a sense of inadequacy. I became critical of my look, accent, and altogether felt agonizingly insecure.

I lived with these erroneous notions and emotions until I made my first friend. He had grown up in the city and was not someone I would typically hang around with or choose as a friend. From afar, one could instinctively tell he was from a wealthy home. His clothes were up to date with the latest fashion, unlike my "old-school" outfits. As he later explained, he drew close because we answered the same first name, enrolled for the same course, and participated actively in the class.

Being appreciated at all and for my contribution to the classwork motivated me to be receptive. So, we kicked up a friendship that would last long after university and for decades. Over time, I discerned that my stylish friend and many others I had deemed perfect had flaws that made them wary. Then, I recognized I had a distorted view of myself and how I thought people judged me.

A clear lesson from my experience is that the feeling of insecurity was psychological and not real. Nevertheless, a sense of insufficiency can be partly due to a lack of skills or competence.

Many of us can relate to Abigail's disposition toward speaking publicly. At the beginning of my professional vocation, I struggled with stage fright and actively avoided addressing a live audience of any magnitude. I remember a particular occasion when my manager sent me a chain of emails about a project that I was leading. The mail contained his conversation with one of the company's directors, and it was about a milestone we achieved. Without my knowledge or consent, my manager had nominated me to present the results at a meeting holding within three weeks.

Leading the project was routine for me but making a presentation at a Department Meeting chaired by the Director was not. Overwhelming anxiety set in because I had never addressed the caliber of people who were to attend the meeting. I did not know what to prepare and how to make the talk worthwhile. The thought that the prospective audience had reviewed countless presentations and knew potential pitfalls was discouraging. I died within by the sword of my insecurity and imagination. Consequently, I admitted defeat, gave up hope, and concluded I had no chance of sharing anything meaningful.

Fortunately for me, the Director called off the meeting just a few days before the scheduled date. I was relieved with the cancellation, but it dawned on me that I had missed an occasion to showcase my competence. My eyes became open to a deficiency in my skills and learning opportunities. I needed a change of attitude towards public speaking if I must thrive on the job. More so, I was nearing a job level in the company's hierarchy where visibility was essential.

When I needed to make a career-critical presentation a few years later, I was ready for a front-stage performance. Since the incident described above, I had come to terms with my deficiencies. I sought God for the grace to face my fears. I researched, attended meetings that I ordinarily would have declined, and paid close attention to presenters.

Over time, I learned how to make my presentation slides captivating and understood the requirements necessary to leave an excellent impression during presentations. The feeling of inadequacy I had previously experienced eventually became a steppingstone for success when it mattered most in my career.

The sense of insufficiency, and the insecurity associated with it, are a reality of life. Feeling inadequate is awful but has a positive side that we can explore. It stirs us to improve where we lack skills and spurs us to explore opportunities for capacity improvement. It keeps us humble, increases our dependency on God, and encourages our affinity to fellow humans.

Do not allow inadequacy to rob you of recovering from adverse situations or pursuing your dreams. Is there a skill, an understanding, or a relationship to develop? Go ahead and acquire it. It will strengthen your inner being and improve your overall outlook. Do not hold back from exploring every possibility to enhance your confidence, including seeking professional counsel if necessary.

Besides, we know that Abigail did not resolve her inadequacies before reaching out and appearing before King Solomon. She did not have the chance to learn the king's protocol or presentation skills because her situation was urgent. Even if Abigail acquired new skills, it is practically impossible to change her past. So, Abigail appeared as she was, vulnerable before the king.

Like Abigail, there are things we cannot change or influence in our lives. There will be times when we need to embrace humility rather than doing anything extraordinary. Having tried our best, let us look beyond the limitations and explore God's sufficiency.

1 Corinthians 1:27-29 says, "God chose the foolish things of the world to shame the wise; God chose the weak things of the world to shame the strong. God chose the lowly things of this world and the despised things—and the things that are not—to nullify the things that are, so that no one may boast before him."

We can trust God with those things that scare us the most. He is aware but never despises our weaknesses. Instead, He uses the imperfections to express His strength.

1. What are the signs and symptoms of inadequacy?

2. In what areas of your life do you experience any of these feelings?

3. Are the symptoms due to a lack of skill and competence, or is it psychological?

4. What steps would you suggest to reverse a sense of insufficiency? At what point will you recommend someone who feels inadequate to seek professional help?

5. Feeling insufficient has demerits. How can we turn it around to our benefit?

BIBLE READINGS

2 Corinthians 12:9-10

Psalms 73:26

Romans 8:39

SEEK | FIND | **GROW IN GRACE**

Chapter 6

POWERED BY PURPOSE

> *"The other woman said, 'No! The living one is my son; the dead one is yours.' But the first one insisted, 'No! The dead one is yours; the living one is mine.' And so they argued before the king."*
> *(1 Kings 3:22)*

s we learned from the previous chapters, knowing the truth provided Abigail the courage to contend for her son. Nevertheless, it was her maternal instincts that compelled her to take control of the situation. It does not matter if it is human or animal; all mothers have a natural tendency to protect their young ones at all costs, even if they must risk their lives.

Abigail's son was in danger, and his chances of survival were contingent on her response. As the mother, confronting her adversary became instinctual because her child - one thing she loved and probably cherished the most - was at stake.

Being a victim comes with its unique energy. Recovery after tragic and life-changing incidents requires more than a piece of useful information. In addition to knowledge, it takes courage and willpower.

We typically weigh the pros and cons of choices before making decisions. However, things can be drastically different when there is an emotional connection to what is at stake. In such cases, we are more likely to be instinctual, more open to taking risks than embracing cautious reasoning. In other words, the energy needed for survival comes naturally when something of significant value or personal meaning is at stake.

Passion is crucial to surviving victimhood and succeeding in our endeavors. An informed victim may struggle, but those with a combination of knowledge and willpower never lack reasons to explore opportunities. They hardly stay passive when there is the slimmest chance to improve their condition.

What generates passion in individuals varies. The emotion does not necessarily come from obligations or things we love to do at a moderate level. Instead, it originates from those things we would gladly invest our resources. Whatever we consider worth dying for energizes us to stand firm in the face of opposition.

Suppose you think back to phenomenal stories of survival you have come across. The captivation is usually the victims' resilience, the willingness to endure hardship, and the determination to make it out alive. We hear of activists who laid down their lives for fairness and social change, scientists who faced death and injury in pursuit of innovation, and soldiers who sacrificed their lives to protect their country's beliefs and ideologies. These are occasions where a sense of purpose gives birth to passion and firm resolution.

My wife, Anthonia, had some experiences while pursuing her dream career that demonstrates how a sense of purpose kindles passion and gives us the willpower to escape the physical, mental, and other restraints of being a victim. Her childhood vision was to provide medical care for the needy. Initially, she considered obtaining a degree in Medicine after getting married but did not pursue the idea because our first child was born about a year after the wedding.

Three years passed, we had a second child, and my job began to demand more of my time. We have always believed in raising our children well and giving them the best. The dilemma was that she could not raise two children in a young family while simultaneously pursuing her career.

We explored different vocations that could suit our situation. We attempted careers in women's fashion, fitness, and beauty therapy. Unfortunately, none of these professions gave Anthonia the satisfaction she craved. While we both cherished the marriage, she was neither comfortable nor fulfilled with her circumstances. It was like a part of her was missing.

Then, in 2011, about 13 years into our marriage, we had a breakthrough. Anthonia had a dream where God revealed she could still fulfill her childhood dream. Our older son was 12, while the younger one was 8. We felt they could be reasonably independent and concluded the time was right to forge ahead.

The new development brought so much joy to our home. Within a few days of reviving her dreams, Anthonia came up with a roadmap. Nevertheless, this new venture gave rise to mixed emotions. On the one hand, we were anxious concerning her ability to cope after being a full-time housewife for more than a decade. On the other hand, we were delighted by the hope for the future.

Subsequently, Anthonia applied and got admission to study Nursing in Australia. The admission letter came in March 2011, while the semester was to resume in January 2012. We were Nigerian citizens but Malaysian residents, meaning we needed a visa to enter Australia.

By October 2011, we had saved sufficient funds and ready to submit the visa applications. Considering the stipulated 4 to 6 weeks processing time, we thought we had enough time to sort things out. It was around this time that we had the first significant setback. Our son accidentally washed his international passport. The document was severely damaged, such that we needed to obtain a new one.

Anxiety set in almost immediately, and emotions ran high. The Nigerian Consulate in Malaysia was some two hours of air travel from where we lived. The end of the processing period was fast approaching, and we were incurring unplanned expenses that could take a hefty toll on our finance. In the end, God showed us mercy as we secured the new passport by mid-November. We suffered no time loss, and the financial toll was just manageable.

We had a sigh of relief after the above incident, but it was not long before we encountered another obstacle. This time, it was the attitude of the Case Officer at the Australian Embassy. She would not communicate or reply to the emails we sent. Around that time, some Africans got involved in fraudulent activities in Malaysia. Consequently, the Embassy imposed extensive background checks for Africans intending to enter Australia. Being a Nigerian national, therefore, did not help our cause.

The six-week processing period passed, and there was no update from the Case Officer. Subsequently, we placed a call to the Consulate and learned she had been on leave, which meant our application was pending until her return. It wasn't pleasant to hear that at all. We could not understand why no one stood in for her while she was away on holiday.

Another couple of weeks passed, and we finally received an email from this Officer. Somehow, she concluded that there were insufficient funds in our bank statement. We asked her to walk us through how she arrived at a different figure, and she obliged. As we crosschecked, we discovered her calculation was wrong. Regardless, she would not take responsibility or apologize for the inconvenience she caused.

The waiting continued until mid-January 2012 when the Case Officer requested afresh some documents we had already presented. It was not comforting, but again, we put sentiment aside and complied.

As the calendar marked January 25 - a week before the resumption date, we took a flight to Kuala Lumpur. Unable to wait any longer, we hoped to visit the Consulate in person, secure the visa, and travel to Australia.

Anthonia scheduled an appointment and visited the Consulate the morning after we arrived. And for the second time, they requested a letter from my employer. At that point, it truly felt as if they were out to frustrate us. Even so, I got the reference anyway and passed it to the Case Officer. We also notified the Embassy of our circumstances. The next day was Friday, and Australian schools were due to resume on Monday.

We had monitored the flights to Australia for weeks but could not make a booking because we were not sure of our fate. We watched as the seats on many flights filled, and flight tickets rose in price. Our faith and patience were tested and stretched. Eventually, at about 3 am on Friday 27, with a nudge of hope from my wife, we summoned the courage to book the flights and scheduled our departure for 10 pm the same day. We had no visa and no sign that anything was heading in the right direction at that moment. It was the case of now or never.

Later that morning, approximately ten hours before the booked flight's departure time, we got a call to pick up our passports. The hotel where we lodged was some ten-minute walking distance to the Australia Consulate. Anthonia rushed there immediately, but they only offered her and the children a visa, to our disappointment. They said I should have applied for a visitor visa rather than a temporary resident permit. The premise was that I was not planning to live with them in Australia but want to continue my job in Malaysia. The news was heartbreaking. We wondered why they left us in the dark until the very last minute.

Still, this was a miracle. There was no time for a pity-party. We had an urgent and vital decision to make, and we had only two options. We could delay the trip by two weeks to process my visa or for Anthonia to travel alone with the kids. Anthonia would not allow the opportunity she had chased with tears for decades to slip away. Nothing would deter her from getting it now that it was within her reach. Hence, she chose to make the journey without me.

While we rejoiced because we accomplished the primary goal, we were sad because I could not participate in the trip. I accompanied Anthonia and the kids to the airport that night. Some seven hours after departure, they landed safely in Australia. It was barely 48hrs before schools were due to resume.

After checking in to the hotel, Anthonia began to collect information about houses in her preferred suburbs. She searched for homes that were available for rent and opened for inspection that weekend. By God's divine guidance, she found one that met her criteria. She inspected it the next day, which was a Sunday, submitted an application to lease it, and got the house. As God would have it, the residence was only a seven-minute walk from the children's school.

I did not join my family in Australia until eight weeks after they traveled. Moreover, within two weeks of arrival, Anthonia settled for a new life in Australia, a country she had never visited. She completed school registration for herself and the kids, leased a house, and bought a car.

All the while, Anthonia took upon her the responsibility to pray for God's intervention in our situation. She was vibrant and intense in prayer during the period. I have always been an intercessor, but her dedication challenged me.

Settling in Australia alone stretched Anthonia to the limits in many areas. She slept late and woke up early, shed tears, prayed like never, and slept on the floor for a few nights before the furniture arrived. She was exhausted but never lacked the zeal for the next step.

I watched the famous saying, "When there is a will, there is a way," play out in Anthonia while chasing her dream. I can confidently attribute her willpower and passion to a vision that promised a sense of purpose. For her, a thing of personal meaning and psychological significance was on the line. Therefore, she took the battle for success very personally, and nothing would stop her from achieving the goal.

Having a sense of purpose will motivate us to thrive in our trades and quickly recover when we suffer setbacks. Notwithstanding, discovering what gives fulfillment is easier for some people than others. Anthonia knew what she wanted to be from childhood, and she knew when she found it. I did not find my passion until I was 25. That was after I accepted Christ as my Lord and Savior.

The above success story took vision, focus, dedication, and a strong belief in divine intervention – attributes exhibited by Abigail.

1. What are the things that trigger passion in you?

2. What do you understand by the word, passivity?

3. Have you ever lacked the energy to intervene in a situation despite having the right information? Share the experience.

4. Why is passion relevant to gaining back control of our lives after a setback?

5. Describe a situation when passion contributed significantly or compelled you (or an associate) to achieve a tangible goal.

BIBLE READINGS

John 12:27-28

Genesis 30:1

Daniel 1:8

SEEK **FIND** **GROW IN GRACE**

Chapter 7

SEEKING DIVINE HELP

"One of them said, 'Pardon me, my lord. This woman and I live in the same house, and I had a baby while she was there with me.'" (1 Kings 3:17)

Abigail was troubled while her son, probably the most important thing in her life, lay in the arms of her former friend, who turned a mortal adversary. Consequently, she took the initiative to contest her case before King Solomon. Abigail rejected passivity and refused to remain a victim while she had reason to believe the situation was salvageable.

To say consulting the king was significant for Abigail to regain her son would be an understatement. She tried dialogue but could not persuade Dinah to hand over the baby. Introducing King Solomon means Abigail brought the king's wisdom and authority into play - the highest recourse available for her mission.

As we now know, Abigail's decision paid off. King Solomon unraveled Dinah's deception, forcing the desperate woman to succumb to superior wisdom and bow out in defeat. Besides, Abigail reunited with her son, and King Solomon received resounding praise from his subjects, and his fame spread abroad for his wise intervention. There was joy in the nation, and most importantly, the episode brought glory to God.

Abigail's yearnings and her conviction of the truth were essential to her breakthrough reward, but she would not have succeeded but for Solomon's mediation. Her evidence was insubstantial before approaching the king. Her defense was weak, and her fate was uncertain. Until Solomon stepped in, Abigail's future was hanging only by a thread.

In the previous chapters, we discussed the danger of being ignorant and lacking passion concerning significant matters. To be deceived and left with no means to recover would have had life-changing consequences for Abigail. If she had not reclaimed her child despite knowing the truth, the thought that she was so naive and unable to prove her case would have haunted her for life. Her conscience would have condemned her, and she would have lived with a sense of failure as a mother. Thanks to God for giving Israel a wise king in the person of Solomon. Praise the Lord also for Abigail's initiative and the courage to step forward instead of yielding to Dinah's deception and blackmail.

Abigail reclaimed what was legitimately hers because she was not complacent but took the initiative after uncovering the truth. Let us make the most of the information and opportunities at our disposal. Let us be prayerfully resourceful and trust in God's justice and vindication as promised throughout the scriptures, for the oppressed ones.

The enemy does not fret, relent, or release his captives merely because they are informed or enthusiastic. Satan is never disturbed by our head-knowledge, regardless of its extent. He is at ease until we act based on sound understanding. On the other hand, the devil cannot withstand an informed Christian who involves God in their struggles.

Jesus demonstrates how we should involve God in our lives through prayers. He never ceased to pray despite knowing God's word from start to the end, and He repeatedly challenged His disciples to take prayer seriously. "On one occasion, while he was eating with them, he gave them this command: 'Do not leave Jerusalem but wait for the gift my Father promised, which you have heard me speak about. For John baptized with water, but in a few days, you will be baptized with the Holy Spirit'" (Acts 1:4-5).

The disciples paid due diligence to the above instruction and reaped a bountiful reward for their obedience. They waited steadfastly in Jerusalem and continued to pray until the day of Pentecost when they received the baptism of the Holy Spirit.

Prayer is a sure means to bring God's promise into our possession. God promised the Holy Spirit and was eager to honor the commitment, but the disciples needed to pray for the gift to materialize. Receiving many of God's promises, be it those in the scriptures or the ones prophesied over us, are contingent on our willingness to ask God to fulfill His word. Believers who undermine prayers may possess only a fraction of what God is willing to provide. God's unconditional will must come to pass, but His conditional will require our cooperation through our prayers.

Samson's story in Judges 15 illustrates how prayer can save a dire situation. It showcases how we can make petitions productive and highlights the joy that awaits those who call on God. Judges 15: 18-19 says, "Because he was very thirsty, he cried out to the Lord, 'You have given your servant this great victory. Must I now die of thirst and fall into the hands of the uncircumcised?' Then

God opened the hollow place in Lehi, and water came out of it. When Samson drank, his strength returned, and he revived. So the spring was called En Hakkore, and it is still there in Lehi."

The above Bible passage paints a picture of what transpired after Samson had a remarkable victory against the Philistines. He became thirsty, cried to God for assistance, and He rescued him. We know that water is a basic need. Apart from air, it is perhaps the most crucial element for life. Without an intervention, Samson was going to die.

Samson was conscious of not being by himself. He knew God gave him strength, ordained the destiny he was pursuing and saw him thus far. So he prayed, seeking help from the One who had the highest stake in his survival.

Samson's prayer touched God's heart in many ways. He began the supplication by talking about the victory that God gave him. He attributed the conquests to God, meaning that his fate would have been different if not for the Lord who favored him. By reminding ourselves and acknowledging His wondrous deeds, we boost our confidence to pray and believe God for the supernatural. There are no hard and fast rules in prayer. But we see a pattern in the scriptures such that people who sought God rendering praises first before making their petitions.

Besides, you must have noticed that Samson presented his request to God in the form of a question. He asked God why He would allow him to die of thirst and fall into the uncircumcised hands. It is absurd for an ordinary human to query his Maker. So, we may consider Samson to be rude in his approach. Nevertheless, such a gesture is possible in dialogues between friends when there is an established cordial relationship.

The content of Samson's question reveals a sound understanding of God's nature and His stake in his life. He petitioned God for reasons why He would allow him to die at the hand of a Philistine. Samson understands that both his death and the circumstance that may lead to it are equally important to God. No responsible father allows a stranger to mistreat their children without a cause. The book of 2 Samuel 12 affirms Samson's understanding of God's interest in how His children die. The passage documents how God disciplined David for having an Israeli soldier (named Uriah) killed by the Philistines.

Samson cried out to God in Lehi, an area recorded to be hollow. The people had come to recognize the place to be empty, accepting its fruitlessness. In response to Samson's prayers, God did the miraculous, creating a spring, an unceasing water source from which Samson drank and refreshed. More so, Samson changed the story and reputation of Lehi for good. No one will ever thirst in Lehi anymore. In other words, anyone who needs refreshing at Lehi could drink and revitalize from this new fountain.

The spring that God opened at Lehi following Samson's prayers was called "En Hakkore," meaning "The spring of him that called" or "The fountain of the crier." The name indicates that our prayers and tears are invaluable, and they leave an impression on God's heart. Samson would have died if he had not prayed. Except for his petition, thirst would have remained the identity of Lehi.

Divine assistance is vital to reaching exceptional heights and fulfilling our potentials. Still, we sometimes fail to recognize or benefit from the opportunity to seek God for it. Before concluding this chapter, let us examine a few examples of missed opportunities due to a lack of persistent prayer.

The book of 2 Chronicles 15 provides details of how King Asa, an ancient king in Judah, pioneered one of Israel's most renowned reformations. He removed the idols from the land, repaired the Lord's altar, and the people eagerly sought God. Asa's reform was so popular that many Northern Kingdom's residents migrated to the South, where Asa was king. To cap it all, God sent words to encourage Asa for his good works from time to time.

Regrettably, "In the thirty-ninth year of his reign, Asa was afflicted with a disease in his feet. Though his disease was severe, even in his illness, he did not seek help from the Lord, but only from the physicians" (2 Chronicles 16:12). The menial ending of King Asa must have broken God's heart. One would have expected him to petition God, but he did not, despite knowing God so intimately. I am confident that Asa's fate would have been different if he sought God in addition to seeking the doctors. God is our Healer. He may work through medical science or directly heal us miraculously.

A personal instance of missed opportunities due to lack of prayers is instructive. I learned a painful lesson in 2004 when the Lord revealed to me in a dream an imminent attack on my family. The period coincided with when I was very engaged with work and church activities. So, I was too busy to pray. A few weeks passed, and what I saw in the dream happened in reality. A couple of weeks later, the Lord revealed in another dream how casually I took the critical issue. Unfortunately, I suffered a considerable loss of money and inconveniences for not paying attention to the first dream.

We will not always feel like praying, sometimes due to laziness or optimistic schedules. The situations we go through may also discourage us from seeking God. At the very least, we should endeavor to find a quiet place and stay silent in God's presence while communing in our hearts. Reading the scriptures and listening to gospel songs may not be direct substitutes for prayer. Nonetheless, they can create the right atmosphere, boost our confidence, and stir our souls to converse with God.

If need be, let us seek support from the community of believers where God placed us. We can benefit from the strength of fellow Christians while we are weak. They can intercede on our behalf and pray with us until we can stand on our own.

There is no formula for praying. As we saw in Samson, our emotional experience can dictate our choices of words and the place where we pray. We need not pretend or worry about the perfect structure while conversing with God. I prefer to pray in a solitary place. My car, often parked in the garage, provides an ideal location with the least distractions. As for my wife, Anthonia, she goes on the treadmill whenever she is under stress and needs divine assistance. The environment helps calm her emotions, and while exercising the physical body, she engages her spirit, supplicating God in deep prayers beyond utterance. The Holy Spirit, who indwells believers, also prays for us when we lack the words.

To receive answers to our prayers, we need personal sincerity and the gracious will of God. God knows the state of our minds and appreciates genuineness more than perfection. 1 Samuel 16:7 says, "…People judge by outward appearance, but the Lord looks at the heart." Let us take courage in the knowledge that Jesus loves us dearly, and He is waiting for us to involve Him in our struggles.

Based on the examples shared so far, we can conclude that knowledge unexercised is unprofitable. A good piece of information is meaningless until we utilize it. Moreover, God is displeased when we suffer unnecessarily. I encourage you not to let anything get in the way of your miracle. Instead, seek God until He turns your situations around for good.

"What a friend we have in Jesus, all our sins and griefs to bear"
"What a privilege to carry everything to God in prayer"
"Oh, what peace we often forfeit, oh what needless pain we bear"
"All because we do not carry everything to God in prayer"

1. Abigail knew the truth and was passionate to recover her son. Regardless, she had no chance to succeed without Solomon's intervention. What does this tell us about involving God when we face life's battles?

2. What would have been Abigail's fate without the king's intervention?

3. Compare the above to a believer who has the best of information and eager but lacks supernatural help to achieve a goal.

4. Do you have a regular time of prayer? What are the things that motivate or discourage us from praying?

5. To receive answers to our prayers, we need personal sincerity and the gracious will of God. Why are these elements very crucial?

BIBLE
READINGS

Matthew
7:7-8

Luke
18:1-6

I Thes.
5:16-18

SEEK | FIND | GROW IN GRACE

Chapter 8

A BRASH DECREE

Then the king said, "Bring me a sword." So they brought a sword for the king. He then gave an order: "Cut the living child in two and give half to one and half to the other." (1 Kings 3:24-25)

I f Abigail thought her struggles were over when she appeared before King Solomon, she must have been disappointed as the court hearing of her dispute with Dinah commenced. After presenting herself as the living child's mother, her adversary took the stand and refuted her claims.

To the king's face and without apology, Dinah accused Abigail of infanticide and insisted the child in contention was her own. After all the arguments, the case remained in a deadlock. At that point, Solomon summed up what he heard from the women and issued a bold judgment - to cut the living child into two and give each woman a piece.

Abigail must have been overwhelmed with disappointment through her battle with Dinah, but nothing would have prepared her for the moment the king ordered his servants to kill the child. She had approached the king to prevent her son from being raised by a strange neighbor. Now it appeared she would be witnessing his gruesome murder.

It is a cardinal rule in a king's court that the king's ruling cannot change. I envisage everyone in Solomon's court braced for the worst as the king's servant appeared with a sword. No one could fathom the king's intention; none could discern the thought in his mind. Except for the king, everyone assumed he had proclaimed his ruling while he only weighed the intent in each woman's heart.

In the wake of Solomon's order, Abigail must have felt like she had failed. Her circumstance demanded to choose between willingly giving away the child she tried so hard to regain in light of a bigger picture or losing him entirely. After all, for another woman to raise the boy is better than for him to be dead.

Abigail must have regretted opting for the king's intervention and assumed it was a big mistake. Unfortunately, or should I say, fortunately, it was too late to withdraw her petition. She would have to see through what she started despite the looming prospect of pain.

Similar to Abigail's case, when we bring petitions before God, His immediate response may sometimes make us want to drop to our knees in anguish. Like Abigail, we are prone to misinterpret God's gesture, thinking He has ruled against us. On the contrary, God, being the righteous Magistrate of heaven, always allowed us the opportunity to demonstrate our genuine intent.

Humans judge one another based on what we can see, while God looks beyond face value and searches deep into our hearts' motives. God may take a Christian through unfamiliar routes but for good reasons. It could be for our good, the benefit of those around us, or to expose the Enemy's craftiness. The path He guides us through may seem callous and uncertain. Nevertheless, He never despises the longing of our souls when it aligns with His heart.

One thing continues to resonate with me concerning Solomon's Court's events, which I urge every believer to remember. While King Solomon ordered his attendants to bring a sword and cut the child in two, his intentions were nothing but the best, and it was superior to what Abigail could achieve by her strength.

In his heart, Solomon had determined to give the boy the chance to gain life in full. Moreover, as flawed and helpless Abigail might have been or felt about herself, the king needed her cooperation to achieve his purpose.

Abigail presumably thought for a moment that the king she sought for vindication had abandoned her. Such a thought is a wrong assumption because God will never forsake His children. Therefore, we should not tolerate such an idea under any circumstance.

Someone may ask, "How could Abigail have discerned the thought in Solomon's heart? How could she have recognized she was safe with the king when every logic concluded her case as ill-fated? Is there any possibility she would have been hopeful despite seeing the messenger of death with the sword?" How do we manage moments when we try our best, and yet the prospect of our situation is doom and gloom? These are questions asked by everyday believers. They form the basis for this chapter's conclusion and the center of the next ones.

First and foremost, we came to know Christ by faith. Though we did not see Him, we believed He is the Almighty who is powerful, compassionate, and faithful enough to handle our affairs. Journeying with Him requires continuing in the same trust upon which we established the relationship. We need to believe His promises, including the famous one in Jeremiah 29:11 that says, "For I know the plans I have for you," declares the Lord, "plans to prosper you and not to harm you, plans to give you hope and a future."

Be rest assured that God will defend your interest regardless of whether He shows signs about your situation or not. He is a just God. "…Anyone who comes to Him must believe that He exists and that He rewards those who earnestly seek Him" Hebrews 11:6.

Moreover, when He deems it fit, God provides His people with hints on their challenges. In both the Old and New Testaments, God gave His children a pre-knowledge and outcome of their circumstances through dreams, visions, and trances. These divine insights helped the people stay firm despite a natural urge to panic.

For example, Joseph, the husband of Mary, had a series of revelations through which God guided him and his family to safety while King Herod plotted against baby Jesus. Again, when Apostle Paul faced fierce opposition in Corinth, God spoke to him in a dream not to be afraid. The Lord further informed him that there were many other believers there. Subsequently, the zealous Apostle knew he was not alone, gained courage, and preached Jesus in the city.

I can also personally testify of the strength received from divine insights. In 2007, while believing God for my employer to send me on an overseas assignment, I got a more hectic role in the same location. I struggled that season and could not comprehend why God allowed me to suffer hardship while I prayed for a motivating job.

Subsequently, I had a dream where I was murmuring inwardly at the office but did not voice my feelings. Then I saw myself in a place that resembled my manager's secretary's office. There, I overheard people whispering to one another about how fortunate I was. They said to each other that the hardship I was going through meant to prepare me for my next job. Then I woke up.

As you can imagine, the insight God gave me through the dream was an eye-opener. It gave me the courage to persevere during the problematic season as it promised light at the end of the tunnel. More so, because the dream is of the Lord, He fulfills what He foretold. And honestly, the experience acquired from the tumultuous period helped me succeed in the next role, which was the overseas assignment I craved.

Abigail's experience at King Solomon's court was scary and traumatic. She might not have pressed for justice if she had foreseen in her wildest dream that the king would at any point give the command to kill her child.

Foreseeing any distress worse than what we are already experiencing can discourage us from chasing our dreams or seeking justice in a victim's case. As a result, God in His mercy may not disclose every piece of information about our situation. He may also motivate us to the point where we have no option but to fight until our breakthrough comes.

I asked my teenage son to share an occasion when he felt let down before knowing the season was for his benefit.

The account below was his response, his perspective of the same event I shared in Chapter 2.

"I struggled and felt disappointed between August 2017 and January 2018. I did not know God allowed the challenge I faced for a good reason. The family had just confirmed the need to relocate from Mount Gambier, a country suburb in South Australia. The plan was to move to Melbourne, Australia's second-largest city."

"I was concerned about adjusting to city life. I thought about getting into a school where I will feel welcomed. Besides, I was anxious about getting into a Basketball club in Melbourne. The clubs in Melbourne are highly competitive. I knew I had to raise my game if I must secure a place."

"While preparing for the challenge ahead, I sustained a severe knee injury that threatened to hold me bound for months. Sports activities were a huge motivation for my studies and mental state. The inability to participate in the games felt like the worst thing that could happen. Then, my relationship with God got tested. I could not cope with the fact that God allowed the single thing that kept me going for years to be taken away."

"By October 2017, some three months after the accident, the Physiotherapist projected I needed five months before returning to physical activities. The family planned to relocate by January 2018. Knowing I would not be strong enough to participate in the clubs' tryouts in Melbourne was devastating. I also stood the risk of not playing any competitive game for an entire year if I missed the trials."

"I continued periodic check-ups with the Physiotherapist but was restless about the future of the game I loved. Without my parent's permission, I contacted a few basketball clubs in Melbourne and exchanged a few emails. To my greatest surprise, I got clearance to return to sport by January 15. Before then, I had received an invitation to try out for Hawthorn Magic, one of the teams I contacted."

"By God's grace, the family arrived in Melbourne just in time for the trials. Fortunately, I performed well, despite only returning from injury. I got admitted to the team, which meant that I could participate in the tournaments, a chance I did not have in Mount Gambier."

"I learned some critical lessons of life and profited from the challenging experience. I am encouraged to trust and rely on God no matter what situation I found myself. I put into practice the understanding that faith without works is dead, and I saw the result. I was barely 15 when this incident happened and considered a minor in Australia. My parents were not happy because I did not carry them along but were impressed by my initiative."

In conclusion, Abigail's day in Solomon's court was rough, but it delivered the expected result. Our situation may take a turn for the worse while seeking God, and it may seem like the Enemy has the upper hand. We should always trust God to cover our back, with or without pre-knowledge of our situation. He does not abandon His people.

1. What is the central point of the chapter?

2. How should we respond to unfavorable situations after seeking God's intervention?

3. Have you experienced a situation when things got worse after praying before they got better? What did you learn from the incident(s)?

4. How can we know God has our interest at heart in every situation?

5. Why would God keep away information relevant to our situation or recovery?

BIBLE READINGS

Hebrews 10: 38-39

Genesis 50:20

Isaiah 63:9

Jeremiah 29:11

SEEK | FIND | GROW IN GRACE

Chapter 9

LOVE FACTOR

bigail petitioned King Solomon to rescue her son from her housemate. During the hearing, the king ordered to kill the child and divide him between the two women. Deeply moved with compassion, Abigail pleaded with Solomon not to harm the boy, but her opponent heartily consented to the king's interim decision.

By asking his servant to bring a sword and cut the child in half, Solomon, by implication, gave the mother the rights to decide the boy's fate. Moreover, the king's call was a test of the spirits at work in the women.

We know God's plan towards us is to have life in abundance while the enemy schemes to steal, kill, and destroy us. The king's tactics made it apparent who was inspired by godly virtues and the person driven by worldly instincts. Like the purification process that differentiates coal from diamonds, the women's true colors showed when they were under intense pressure. One revealed utter desperation and recklessness, while the other exhibited compassion and self-control.

Abigail managed the surprise of the king's decree quite well. She remained focused on the purpose for which she sought the king's attention, which is to save the boy. After enduring so much in her pursuit, it would have been disappointing if she approved of his proposed death.

Abigail's choice to allow her rival to raise the child was a sensible compromise. If the king allowed her request, the baby would live. There could even have been a likelihood of reuniting with the child in the future. On the contrary, the baby's death would be of no gain to anyone. Furthermore, Abigail's response was selfless, a reflection of her core values and character. She put the baby's interest ahead of hers, proving the child occupied a special place in her heart and more precious than her self-esteem.

Love for her son was the motivation behind Abigail's pursuit of justice and her attitude during the trial. Compassion compelled her to cry for intervention and made her plead for mercy when the boy's life was in danger. She suffered provocation and discomfort along the way. Nonetheless, she did not cease to show genuine love and self-control, an integral part of the Holy Spirit's fruit.

Abigail had reasons to be mad at Solomon after he appeared emotionally insensitive with his initial solution, which seemed to favor the offender. She could have cursed the king and faced the penalty. After all, the child she loved dearly was about to die through a hasty judgment. A lack of self-control or a stupid response at that moment would have obscured the truth and created more confusion. It would have prevented justice and hindered her breakthrough regardless of the king's ability and eagerness to assist. Her outburst could have led to her death but orphan the boy. Several alternate scenarios could have resulted from an unguarded moment driven by emotion.

All in all, a failure to express compassion for the baby would have indicated Abigail's lack of appreciation for his life. Without godly traits, it would have been challenging, if not impossible, to prove she deserved to keep the child.

We contribute to our fate

King Solomon gave Abigail the chance to decide her fate in the darkest hour when the battle raged most fiercely. God is sovereign, yet He allows us the free will to choose on some matters concerning us. We contribute to our destiny's outcomes, both deliberately and subconsciously. Therefore, let us be sensitive and make positive input into our future as we go about our daily affairs.

Abigail's case proves how much God needs our cooperation to help us. If she had not established compassion for the baby, Solomon might not have allowed her to have him. The king may have spared the child's life but sent him to a foster parent. Without undermining God's omniscient nature and His power to discern all things, our actions can hinder a breakthrough despite His willingness to bless us.

Abigail's story exemplifies how our actions impact the people around us, notably the vulnerable who look up to us for guidance and protection. Her self-image was at risk in her choice, but the child's entire life was in jeopardy if she had chosen otherwise. The implications of our decisions may become more meaningful when we realize what is at stake for others.

Abigail was in desperate need. She knew the truth about her circumstance and hoped for the king's right discernment. Even with all these qualities, including a raw passion for success, Abigail would have failed in her pursuit if she had not shown love and self-control during the fierce battle.

Love and war are miles apart in meaning. They are two words that appear to have nothing in common. Yet, love is essential for victory, be it in spiritual warfare or physical battles. Are you in a contest and desire victory? Do you want safety and deliverance for yourself, your loved ones, or an associate? Clothe yourself with the garment of love. It will secure you the victory you crave. Moreover, you will avoid hurting yourself or the people you are trying to protect. In today's world, where the end often justifies the means, we should learn from this timeless story that good trumps evil in the final analysis.

Be guided, dear friends. Let love never leave you, be it in a time of peace or during challenges. Bind it around your neck, write it on the tablet of your heart. Then you will be upright and win favor in the sight of God and man. Love is essential to gaining victory in any form of warfare because it puts us in the same perspective with the Lord and strengthens our position in Him.

To be devoted to Christian values is prudent and advantageous. God looks beyond outward appearances. He searches our hearts for the motives behind the petitions. "For the eyes of the Lord range throughout the earth to strengthen those whose hearts are fully committed to him..." 2 Chronicles 16:9.

1. Why is love crucial to winning physical or spiritual battles?

2. What are the potential consequences of a lack of self-control or a stupid response during physical or spiritual battles?

3. In the light of the scriptures, why is love so important to God?

4. Share the experience of an occasion when love brought about victory or reconciliation.

5. How do we maintain composure in dire situations?

BIBLE READINGS

Matthew 22:36-40

Romans 13:9-10

SEEK | **FIND** | **GROW IN GRACE**

Chapter 10

DANGER OF RETRIBUTION

"The woman whose son was alive was deeply moved out of love for her son and said to the king, 'Please, my Lord, give her the living baby! Do not kill him!' But the other said, 'Neither I nor you shall have him. Cut him in two!'" (1 Kings 3:26)

While King Solomon gave the order to cut Abigail's child in two, Dinah agreed, but Abigail begged the king to spare the little child. Abigail's plea shows that her love for the boy surpasses the grudge against Dinah and the king who gave the brash decree. If her disposition were contrary, she possibly would have chosen revenge and concurred that the child should die to deny her adversary an undue advantage. That would have been myopic and borne out of vengeance, which often obscures sensible judgment.

Victims can face the temptation to resent those who purposely cause them harm and despise those who failed to prevent them from anguish. It is vital to avoid letting the anger against the enemy dominate our thoughts and actions. If not, the resentment can overshadow the love for ourselves and our loved ones and impede our progress in life.

In the early chapters, we encouraged victims to seek justice through appropriate means. Pursuing justice is lawful, evidence-based, fair, and void of conflicts of interest. The reverse is when victims take the law into their hands because they feel the law is too lenient, and the offender deserves a more significant penalty.

Reprisal goes beyond holding people accountable for their conduct. It is a desire to punish those who wronged us. To avenge oneself is not a smart option; it is morally wrong and unlawful. Those who seek revenge are mostly emotion-driven and are likely to overreact, overstep moral boundaries, and become cruel.

Vengeance may promise emotional release and immediate satisfaction, but it does not guarantee closure to whatever matter we aim to resolve. Revenge is not cheap. Often, people regret the decision to avenge themselves. Besides, it can extend conflicts and make them spiral into a cycle of retaliation.

God warns us against retribution; it is a sin before Him. The scriptures say in Romans 12:19, "Do not take revenge, my dear friends, but leave room for God's wrath, for it is written: 'It is mine to avenge; I will repay,' says the Lord." Therefore, let us exercise restraint and shun the urge to avenge ourselves. Such actions demonstrate a lack of faith in God and His ability to grant us justice against our adversary.

There was a soccer match where both teams were desperate to win. So, the atmosphere in the stadium was tense from kickoff. The situation worsened as the game progressed into the second half and neared the final whistle. Suddenly, one of the teams had an opening for a counterattack. To prevent the last-second loss to their rivals, a defender tackled the opposing striker as he charged towards the goal. Though the tackle was intentional and unfair, anyone who assessed the situation without prejudice would agree that it didn't quite endanger the striker's safety. The referee was about to intervene when the striker suddenly proceeded to assault the defender who tackled him.

The reaction of the fans was swift and immediate. The stadium went into an uproar, and the teams' supporters engaged themselves in heated arguments and altercations. Everyone claimed their team was innocent and blamed the other. In the end, the referee issued the defender a yellow card as a caution for his tackle. Meanwhile, the striker who retaliated with a punch received a straight red card, an outright dismissal from play for unlawful misconduct. The striker's team, now playing with ten men, struggled after this incident. They were demoralized after losing a man and eventually lost the game.

In the above example, the referee judged the individuals without prejudice. He disciplined the players based on their actions and according to the rules of the game. For the striker who avenged himself, he and his team paid a hefty price for his lack of self-control. He came into the game as a substitute to strengthen his squad but ended up costing his team the desired win. As you can imagine, he became very unpopular among fans after the incident. Further, had he controlled his temperament despite the offending tackle, he may have won his team a precious free kick that could have led to victory for his team. He lost everything by his rash reaction.

There will always be a temptation to be selfish and self-centered when under pressure. Satan would present our situation as a lonesome struggle against the world. Let us be diligent and avoid extreme measures borne out of desperation. Such actions will harm innocent people and will do us no good. It is inappropriate to make the innocent suffer because we are in distress.

We can become despairing when faced with difficulty. The situation can worsen if left unchecked. To a sound mind, there can never be a justification for an innocent child to die. Still, when caught in conflict with a firm rival, Dinah supported ending the baby's life to satisfy her conceit.

God is not partial. He is a righteous judge who rules in fairness and judges according to our deeds. When people wrong us, God holds them accountable. If we unjustly punish those who offend us, their soul will cry out to God, who will hold us responsible for any unjust acts.

1. What are the possible reasons why people avenge themselves?

2. Under what circumstance have you been tempted to retaliate?

3. What are the risks of seeking retribution?

4. Why should we allow God to avenge us? Provide answers from the viewpoints of an offender and a victim.

5. Have you heard of "The laws of war," or "International humanitarian law"? Why do such laws exist even in a secular world?

BIBLE READINGS

Leviticus 19:18

Romans 12:19

Matthew 16:27

SEEK | **FIND** | **GROW IN GRACE**

Chapter 11

THE KING'S STAKE

Then the king said, "Bring me a sword." So they brought a sword for the king. He then gave an order: "Cut the living child in two and give half to one and half to the other." (1 Kings 3:24-25)

After Abigail examined the dead child by her side, she knew Dinah had deceived her without a doubt. Before involving King Solomon, she recognized she was embarking on a just cause despite the weak evidence.

The king's command to cut the living child in two would make anyone in Abigail's position wary. And for her opponent to concur with Solomon must have increased Abigail's feeling of isolation drastically. Regardless, Abigail would be wrong if she thought she was the only person concerned about the boy's life. The king probably had a higher stake.

While introducing this book, we discussed how Solomon offered sacrifices and how the Lord asked him to request anything he desired subsequently. The incident was a personal conversation, and it is unlikely anyone knew God had granted Solomon wisdom without measure. So, while Abigail entered Solomon's court, thinking she was all alone, God had equipped the king with the discretion and authority to vindicate her.

Solomon's stake in Abigail's matter was high for many reasons. The reward for the thousands of burnt offerings, the essence of prayers for wisdom, and God's yearning for righteousness among His people were all at risk.

The king's integrity was on the line too. If he were to judge wrongly and the truth later became known to the public, they would doubt his competence. In essence, while someone might presume Abigail's matter was ordinary, there were profound implications for her, her beloved son, King Solomon, and God.

Abigail wasn't aware she was seeking compassion from a king who could empathize with her pains. I doubt if she knew Solomon was once in a dilemma like hers. A few years before he became king, one of his brothers had attempted to take advantage of the sensitive period before his inauguration and effectively started a coup. It took God's intervention to frustrate the conspiracy.

Abigail entered Solomon's court feeling insignificant and vulnerable. While her isolation was real, intimately knowing the king, whom she desperately looked up to for comfort, would have helped her emotions and confidence. I wish Abigail realized beforehand that Solomon was able and had her best interest at heart. The understanding would have aided her composure as she commenced her recovery journey. On the other hand, she would have suffered anxiety unnecessarily if the truth eluded her.

Greater than Solomon is here

Like Abigail, sometimes we worry if our case is redeemable, especially when we lack concrete evidence to support our claims or because of the enemy's intimidation. Knowing God intimately and understanding His kind nature towards His children will motivate us to approach the throne of grace with confidence.

King Solomon's stakes were high in Abigail's matter. Higher still is Jesus's stake in ours. Jesus's sacrifice is more significant than Solomon's. While Solomon offered animals as offerings, Jesus laid down His life. A billion burnt offerings are incomparable to Christ. Consequently, we have a better premise to obtain God's favor in a considerable measure than what Abigail had in Solomon.

Furthermore, greater compassion awaits us in Christ. "For we do not have a high priest who is unable to empathize with our weaknesses..." Jesus, though equal with God, came into the world in the flesh. He lived among us, experienced hunger, and faced temptations. Our redeemer knows what it feels to be bereaved and was a victim of unwarranted violence. He tasted rejection and humiliation. He can relate to our situations and will not relent until he brings justice to those who seek Him.

When Abigail's wisdom fell short, Solomon came to her rescue. So, it is fair to say Abigail triumphed over her accuser in the shadow of the wise king. The good news is that the anointing vested on Jesus for good judgment is much superior to Solomon's. The king displayed only a shadow of the riches in Christ, the Savior in whom all treasures of wisdom and knowledge reside.

Dear friend, we can boast in Jesus, the omniscient advocate. Paul the Apostle described Him in 1 Corinthians 1:30 as, "Wisdom from God—that is, our righteousness, holiness, and redemption." Meanwhile, Jesus referred to Himself as "greater than Solomon" Matthew 12:42.

God's stake in us is invaluable. The reasons behind this are the subject of the next chapter. In the meantime, let us approach God with confidence, knowing we are His inheritance and adopted children through our Lord, Jesus Christ.

1. What is the central message of the chapter?

2. Why was Abigail's vindication so crucial to King Solomon?

3. Compare and contrast Solomon's sacrifice to that of our Lord, Jesus Christ.

4. How does Solomon's stake in Abigail compare to our Lord's stake in us?

5. What should be our attitude towards God for His demonstrated stake in us?

BIBLE READINGS

Deuteronomy 1:31

Jeremiah 31:3

Psalms 8:4-8

Titus 2:14

SEEK | **FIND** | **GROW IN GRACE**

Chapter 12

VALUE OF HUMANS

Then the king gave his ruling: "Give the living baby to the first woman. Do not kill him; she is his mother." (1 Kings 3:27)

To an outsider, Abigail and Dinah's contest ended after King Solomon proclaimed his verdict and the child returned safely to the rightful mother. For Abigail and Dinah, sadly, the trouble was far from over. Regardless of who won the child's custody, the women would have left the court crushed. Their reputations must have been in doubt, and they would have required ample time to heal.

Abigail must have wondered why Dinah, a close associate with whom she celebrated pregnancy and child delivery, turned around to be an adversary. As for Dinah, the thought that she killed her child, betrayed Abigail's trust, stole a child, and denied the act until the king found out must have been devastating.

The news of Abigail and Dinah's encounter must have traveled far and wide. As we all know, such stories can spread very fast. In a real-life situation, some people identify easily with victims while others empathize with the offenders. Abigail and Dinah must have found themselves famous for the wrong reasons, and it is unlikely that both women settled or continued to be friends after the showdown.

It is never easy to put a bold face on when the situation dictates otherwise. To have much going on for us at a point and suddenly hit rock bottom can be disheartening. Therefore, it is natural to struggle with self-esteem after a traumatic experience. As we recognized in Abigail and Dinah's case, a victim and the assailant may both find it difficult to cope after a life-altering experience.

This chapter provides us with the basis to maintain self-esteem and hope after a devastating experience. We will look at reasons to hold fast rather than burying our heads in the sand after an irreversible loss. God wants us to recover. He desires we heal and learn from our mistakes instead of living in despair.

Knowing the worth of humanity, especially from God's viewpoint, can boost our self-confidence. Understanding that our worth does not depend on prevailing physical or emotional state can facilitate hope after setbacks.

I developed an interest in the worth of humanity after visiting a friend some years back. As I gave attention to his two daughters aged between seven and ten, they showcased their talents. The girl who attended ballet classes delivered a spirited performance as if she had been waiting for an opportunity to impress me. The other girl who was learning gymnastics also stopped at nothing to display her abilities.

The competition for my attention became fierce between the sisters when they noticed I complimented the other sibling. As the contest continued, I realized the urge to compete for recognition and prove self-worth does not stop with little children. It can extend into adulthood and last a lifetime, though in different forms. However, when we do not achieve the desired recognition, the painful experience of perceived rejection can be emotionally crushing. There is nothing wrong with demonstrating our talents, but it is essential not to use accolades or acceptance as the standard to measure our worth.

It is acceptable when subjective opinions influence judgments in trivial issues but not in important matters like our inborn worth as human beings. For various reasons, the value of a commodity in a supermarket may fluctuate. Those prices often depend on demand and supply dynamics. Again, the products do have expiry dates, and they have no eternal value beyond the shelf life. As we will learn going forward, humans are priceless. We have lasting value, and our worth is equal and remains the same regardless of age, race, or abilities, etc. We do not fluctuate in value like a bottle of milk in grocery stores that can be the full price today and a half-price the next!

A logical approach to establish an object's value is to consider the materials used, the process involved, and the maker's reputation. We may also determine the value of an item by its utility. To know humans' true nature and worth, we must seek God, the Creator of humanity, for the reasons and elements for and from which He made us. The following insights, mostly based on the scriptures, show how much God values us.

The Almighty God is our Creator

Genesis 2:7 says, "Then the Lord God formed a man from the dust of the ground and breathed into his nostrils the breath of life, and the man became a living being." This Bible passage establishes that God, the Maker of the heavens and earth, created us. This open revelation alone sends a strong message concerning our relevance.

It is easy to perceive the worth of a car in a showroom when you know its brand. If it's a Porsche, your expectation of the quality and value will be high because Porsche's utility is widely known for superiority, and it has a reputation for luxury. Besides, when wealthy and talented architects make designs to showcase their glory, it is always top-notch.

The works of God during creation and nature speak for Him. The universe reflects His greatness. Like the starry hosts' flawless designs, God made humans entirely for Himself. He created us to proclaim His praise (Isaiah 43:21). Therefore, humankind is inestimable in value because of our Creator and the purpose for which He made us.

The Breath of God is in us

The Genesis 2:7 passage we referenced earlier also reveals the item from which God formed humanity. The Bible says we are formed from the dust and by the Breath of God, the Breath that gives us life, making us a living being. Knowing that dust alone has no significant value, we can confidently attribute humanity's worth to the Breath God breathed into us at creation. When we come to terms with the priceless value of God's Breath, which is the Holy Spirit, we can begin to appreciate our actual worth in God's sight. In other words, the fact that we can carry the Spirit of God inside us makes us of infinite value.

God created us in His image

Genesis 1:26 says, "Then God said, let us make mankind in our image, in our likeness, so that they may rule over the fish in the sea and the birds in the sky, over the livestock and all the wild animals, and over all the creatures that move along the ground." The following verse, Genesis 1:27, says, "So God created mankind in his own image, in the image of God he created them; male and female he created them."

You probably notice some similarities in the above Bible passages, yet, it is not a repetition. Genesis 1:26 provides us with God's intention and His conceptual design for humans, while the following verse (Genesis 1:27) reveals the final product.

We are not what we are by chance, and we did not come to be by mistake. A thought process, a plan, and a purpose went into the identity and essential character we manifest today. God designed humans according to His specifications, in His image. He created us to reveal Him, not by accident, but according to His good pleasure and purpose.

While everything God made at creation was good, none has God's personal touch that is so explicitly clear as with human beings. Every human being has a soul and possesses a spirit like God. We have a thought process superior to all other creatures and can make logical decisions. It may be mind-blowing, but God indeed created us in His image and after His likeness. What we have done with all that capacity and potential is beyond the scope of this book. But it is worthy of a pause for some reflection.

The authority vested on us is mighty

The authority that God conferred on humanity, our capability, is incredible. Genesis 1:28 says, "God blessed them and said to them, 'Be fruitful and increase in number; fill the earth and subdue it. Rule over the fish in the sea and the birds in the sky and over every living creature that moves on the ground.'"

We will need to examine what happened before the above declaration to comprehend the vastness of our dominance. God had worked for five days and created everything. On the sixth day, He made man and gave him dominion over His entire works. God gave us authority over animals that lived in the waters, those whose abode is in the air, and those on the ground.

Glorious riches of the One who loves us

The evidence presented so far concerning humanity's worth is from the Old Testament. It is good to know that the New Testament follows a similar pattern and buttresses our infinite value. John 3:16 says, "For God so loved the world that he gave his one and only Son, that whoever believes in him shall not perish but have eternal life." The above Bible passage reveals the depth of God's admiration toward us and our worth. The love lavished on humans must have unsettled some angles! We are that special.

The value of a thing can be determined by who owns or adores it. For example, Catherine Middleton, the wife of Prince William, the Duke of Cambridge, grew up in England. Before 2011 when she got married to Prince William, she worked with her family. The value or worth attributed to her at that stage was nothing compared to when she got married to Prince William. Her financial and social value increased astronomically because of the one who loved her. The same is true of us as humans. We received infinite worth because of the One who loves us. In other words, the priceless value of God who loves us rubs-off on us positively.

Hefty price paid but salvation made easy

Three things made the salvation of humans astonishing. Firstly, the opportunity to repent and be forgiven of our sins. When Satan and many other angels rebelled against God, they had no chance to repent but were banished forever from His presence. Some of them have been in chains since then and until Judgement Day (ref: Jude 1:6). It is noteworthy that God gave humans a second chance after sinning through Adam.

Secondly, the pleasant surprise about humans' salvation is the sacrifice God made, the length to which He went to save humans from perishing. After Adam sinned, God, in His pleasure, sent His Son Jesus to reconcile the broken relationship. Jesus left heaven's glory, came into the world, lived among us in the flesh, despised, rejected, accused, and eventually died a shameful death on a cross.

Is it not appalling that God allowed His Son, who did not sin, to pay the wages for humans' sins? "Very rarely will anyone die for a righteous person, though someone might dare to die for a good person. But God demonstrates his own love for us in this: While we were still sinners, Christ died for us" (Romans 5:7-8 paraphrased).

You can determine how much someone values a thing by what they are ready to sacrifice for it and what they would gladly give away to redeem it. In a practical sense, you can only purchase a thing if you would rather have it instead of the money in your wallet! The extent that God went to save us reveals how much He values us.

It is humbling to read from 1 Peter 1:18-19 that says, "For you know that it was not with perishable things such as silver or gold that you were redeemed from the empty way of life handed down to you from your ancestors, but with the precious blood of Christ, a lamb without blemish or defect."

Finally, the striking thing about our salvation is how easy God made it. One would expect that since God paid a hefty price, the journey to redemption will be torturous and demanding so that humans can appreciate the cost. Surprisingly, God made our salvation free and easy. All that is required to receive salvation is to repent of our sins, confess Jesus as Lord and believe God that raised Him from the dead.

The Almighty God is our Father

One of the most profound privileges Jesus granted humanity is a new level of intimacy with God. We have a closeness that did not exist in the Old Testament. Romans 8:15 says, "…The Spirit you received brought about your adoption to sonship. And by him, we cry, 'Abba, Father.'" Through Christ, every human has the potential to receive the spirit of sonship.

God values us so much that we could be called His sons and daughters. He made Himself directly accountable for us, and we can have a direct fellowship with Him. God's love for us is profound such that He deems it necessary that our well-being and waking moments are His duty.

We are the heir of God's kingdom

By human standards, we measure someone's worth by what they own or stand to inherit. For instance, Princess Charlotte, the daughter of Prince William of the United Kingdom, is estimated to worth 5 billion dollars by her third birthday. As a child, Charlotte cannot have worked a single day at that age. Charlotte can only be worth so much because she is Prince William's daughter.

In the manner Charlotte obtains value through her bloodline, every human can derive value as God's child. We can be God's heirs; we may inherit His kingdom that is of inestimable value. According to 1 Peter 1:4, the inheritance kept for us is neither perishable nor subject to corruption.

In conclusion, while the world may have different rules for measuring values, ours is not a contestable matter in God's mind. He has inherently endowed us with an infinite worth before the foundation of the earth. Today's society may have put in place systems that ascribe value to a few who enjoy special privileges. Such systems are weak and flawed. They are based on trivial matters and have neglected our nature and our Maker's immutable worth, which give humans significance.

God loves and values every human alike, regardless of anything we may experience in the flesh. It is a misconception when we preferentially value ourselves or others based on abilities, age, race, natural talent, or accomplishment. These things lack eternal value and do not determine our true worth. As long as we have God's Breath in us, we are of inestimable worth.

1. Most people easily empathize with victims like Abigail. Under what circumstances will you sympathize with an offender like Dinah? Why should we support the habilitation efforts for offenders?

2. Give reasons (3 each from the Old and New Testament) why humans are of inestimable value regardless of age, race, or social status.

3. What factors make human salvation unique?

4. Based on the scriptures, what is God's ultimate plan for humans?

5. Knowing a human's worth in God's sight, what should be our disposition towards serving others?

BIBLE READINGS

Genesis 2:7

Genesis 1:26-28

Psalms 8:4-8

John 3:16

John 10:10

SEEK **FIND** **GROW IN GRACE**

CONCLUSION

Now let us recap what we have discussed so far, especially the notable lessons. Abigail and Dinah were two vulnerable housemates. They probably supported each other through everyday challenges until disaster struck without warning. Initially, only Dinah suffered a loss. Presumably, due to fear and anxiety, she victimized her unsuspecting neighbor. From that time forward, both women embarked on a battle for survival, each woman for herself.

Abigail was not a superwoman but an everyday mother who faced a typical situation. After running into a problem with her housemate, she carefully examined the issue, embraced the resources available, took the obvious steps, and got the best possible result.

Abigail's victory did not come without a battle. Many factors threatened to thwart her purpose, but she persevered and remained focused until King Solomon vindicated her.

The resources Abigail needed to survive as a victim came naturally. She did not create the morning light that inspired the first glimpse of hope or cause the sun to shine when she needed it. Besides, Abigail did not crown Solomon a king over Israel, and neither did she give him the wisdom to exercise justice. God made all these provisions, and they were readily available before Abigail had the problem.

Moreover, God did not perform a wonder or miracle to liberate Abigail because it was unnecessary. Instead, He allowed the matter to take its natural course while the women dictated their fates based on individual responses to the situation.

A cautious approach would have limited Dinah's regret to losing her child, but a poor judgment worsened her pain. Who knows how she would have fared if she acted wisely and calmly? We can only imagine how God would have comforted her without raising the child from the dead.

Life is good but can present serious challenges, from strained relationships to the loss of loved ones, financial obstacles, health concerns, and so on. Every human will have their share of tough times. The seasons often make our strength visible, test our faith, reveal our character, and show areas where we lack grace.

The values we have developed, the bonds formed with people around us, and the trust built on God dictate how we respond when under pressure. Moreover, our approach to challenges determines whether we will come out triumphantly or not.

If Abigail had not responded in the manner she did and showed love, King Solomon would not have been able to help her. God's sovereignty does not negate human responsibility. Let us reject passivity whenever we can improve our situation. Let us explore the resources God has made available to us. With some effort and determination, we can recover from the enemy's assault and thrive in this life. God can do all things by Himself but chose to work with humans. The readiness to cooperate with Him will significantly improve our chances of winning life's battles.

On a final note, I urge you never to give up trusting God during difficult times. Do not abandon the struggle or admit defeat until you have explored all the options. Like any reasonable father, God may not approve all our petitions because His thoughts are superior to ours. Whenever He denies us a thing, He satisfies us with something much better.

We encourage you to share your thoughts and reactions through our website: www.gleaninggodsfield.org